Monkey PARTY

Rob Waring, *Series Editor*

HEINLE
CENGAGE Learning

Australia • Brazil • Japan • Korea • Mexico • Singapore • Spain • United Kingdom • United States

T0052124

Words to Know

This story is set in Thailand. It happens in Lopburi (lʌpburi), a town north of Bangkok. People and things from Thailand are called 'Thai.'

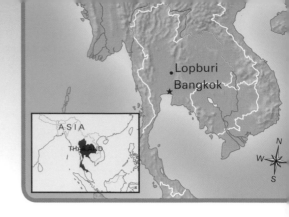

A **Things in Lopburi.** Read the sentences. Label the pictures with the underlined words.

A banquet is a very big dinner, with lots of food.
A cake is something sweet to eat.
A festival is a big, public party.
A monkey is a small animal.
A shrine is a place that is related to a god.

1. _____

2. _____

3. _____

4. _____

5. _____

B **Buddhism.** Read the paragraph. Then complete the definitions with the words in the box.

Buddhists believe in the teachings of a special man named 'Buddha.' Buddhists have many traditions. One Buddhist tradition is to give food to monkeys. This is because of a famous legend. In this legend, a monkey was a hero. Because of this, Buddhists think helping monkeys will bring them good karma. They think good karma will bring them happiness.

Buddhist	hero	karma	legend	tradition

1. Good _____ is a good feeling or kind of luck.

2. A _____ is the main good person in a story.

3. A _____ is a way of doing things year after year.

4. A _____ is a story from a long time ago.

5. A _____ is a person who believes in the teachings of Buddha.

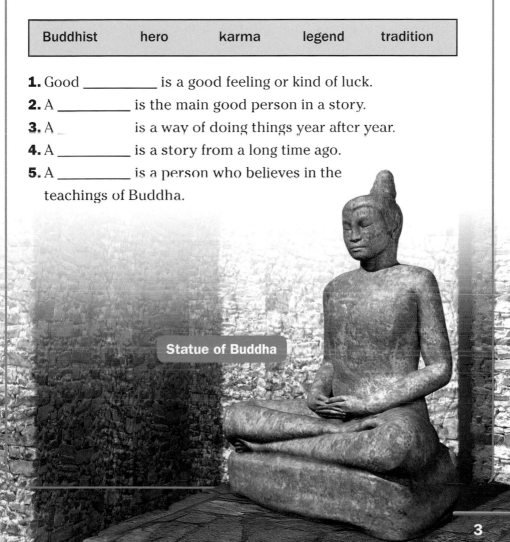

Statue of Buddha

In the town of Lopburi, Thailand, there are monkeys everywhere. They run around the streets. They climb on cars, houses, and other buildings. They can go anywhere they want to, and they get into everything!

The monkeys in this town are very playful and sometimes they cause a lot of trouble. But what about the people of Lopburi? How do they feel about these **mischievous**[1] little animals?

---

[1]**mischievous:** playful in a partly bad way; troublesome

 CD 1, Track 05

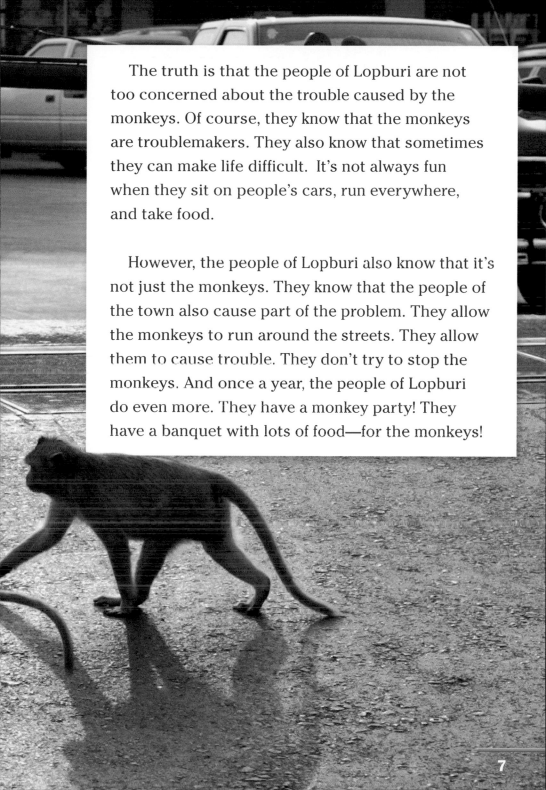

The truth is that the people of Lopburi are not too concerned about the trouble caused by the monkeys. Of course, they know that the monkeys are troublemakers. They also know that sometimes they can make life difficult. It's not always fun when they sit on people's cars, run everywhere, and take food.

However, the people of Lopburi also know that it's not just the monkeys. They know that the people of the town also cause part of the problem. They allow the monkeys to run around the streets. They allow them to cause trouble. They don't try to stop the monkeys. And once a year, the people of Lopburi do even more. They have a monkey party! They have a banquet with lots of food—for the monkeys!

But why do they have this big monkey party? Why do they present the monkeys with a banquet? The reason involves legend and tradition. Most people in Thailand are Buddhists, and for many of them monkeys are very important animals. Monkeys appear in many Thai stories and legends. Because of one special story, some Thai people consider monkeys to be heroes.

In Thailand, there is a famous old legend about a monkey hero named **Hanuman**.[2] In the story, a **demon**[3] takes the god Rama's wife. The monkey Hanuman helps to save Rama's wife. Because of this, Hanuman becomes a hero.

---

[2] **Hanuman:** (hʌnʊmɑn)
[3] **demon:** a bad spirit

Hanuman

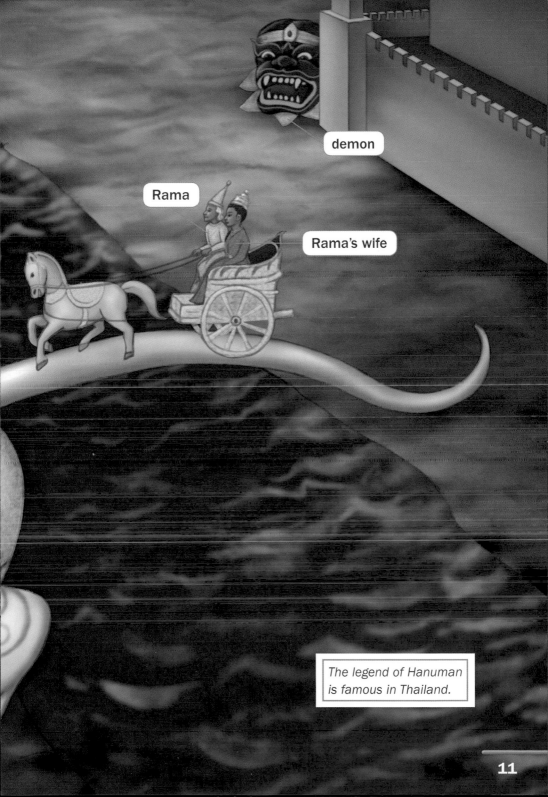

The legend of Hanuman
is famous in Thailand.

Due to the legend of Hanuman and Buddhist traditions, many people in Thailand are still especially kind to monkeys today. This kindness is not limited to allowing monkeys to do anything they wish. Monkeys also get special food often—not just at festivals.

Every day of the year, people bring food for the monkeys to shrines. These people think it's good karma to give them food. The people also think that it will bring them good luck. With this special treatment, the monkeys of Lopburi are getting bigger and bigger all the time!

Fact Check

1. Why do Thai Buddhists like monkeys?

2. What do Thai people do because they like the monkeys?

3. What's happening to the monkeys because of this?

The time for the yearly monkey party finally arrives. It's a time when the community of Lopburi can show the monkeys just how much they like them. They always give the monkeys a lot of special foods at this time. But this year there's a particularly special treat. The festival organizers are giving the monkeys a whole cake!

An organizer of the event explains the banquet and the Buddhist traditions. He says: "Every year there are a lot of people who come and help with the monkey banquet. We want people to help offer food to the monkeys. This is because these monkeys are part of our local Buddhist tradition."

What about this year's cake? Well, it's a very big one, and a lot of people help to make it. The festival organizer explains: "This year, we've made a cake that is **four meters**[4] long for the monkey banquet. Fifty people worked to make this cake. We all wanted to find out if the monkeys liked the cake." Will the monkeys like the cake? Will they want to eat it all?

───────────────────────

[4]**four meters:** 13.12 feet

MONKEY PARTY FESTIVAL

Scan for Information

Scan pages 16 and 17 to answer these questions.

1. Do many people want to help make the cake?

2. How long is the cake?

3. How many people worked to make the cake?

At last, the festival organizers give the monkeys the cake. They don't just like the cake, they love it! The people of Lopburi are very happy and this year's Monkey Party is a big success.

Maybe the people of Lopburi will get good karma because they've treated the monkeys well and given them this beautiful cake. Maybe they won't. Either way, the people of this Thai town did learn one thing—if you want to have a great party for monkeys, give them cake!

After You Read

1. In Lopburi, mischievous monkeys are _____.
   A. anything
   B. everywhere
   C. anywhere
   D. everything

2. Which is NOT a reason why the monkeys are troublemakers?
   A. They sit on cars.
   B. They are heroes.
   C. They get into everything.
   D. They take food.

3. Why are people part of the monkey problem?
   A. because they worry too much
   B. because they make life difficult
   C. because they know that the monkeys cause trouble
   D. because they allow the monkeys to be mischievous

4. How many times in one year do people in Lopburi have a monkey banquet?
   A. three
   B. two
   C. one
   D. doesn't say

5. On page 10, 'this' refers to:
   A. saving Rama's wife
   B. being a monkey
   C. being a demon
   D. the legend

6. What is a good heading for page 10?
   A. The Legend of the Fat Monkey
   B. Monkey Hero Saves Rama's Wife
   C. Monkeys Make Life Difficult
   D. Thailand's Important Party

7. On page 12, the writer's purpose is:
   A. to teach a legend about a monkey
   B. to show why people are nice to the monkeys
   C. to explain why monkeys like cake
   D. to show that the monkeys are getting smaller

8. Some Buddhist people give food to monkeys because they believe each of these EXCEPT:
   A. the legend of Hanuman
   B. the monkeys are special
   C. it's good karma
   D. the monkeys are too big

9. Why do the festival organizers like the monkeys?
   A. because they eat cake
   B. because they are part of tradition
   C. because the party is fun
   D. because many people come

10. _____ people come to help make the cake for the monkey banquet.
    A. No
    B. A lot of
    C. Much
    D. One hundred

11. On page 18, the word 'thing' means:
    A. word
    B. piece of information
    C. way to make a cake
    D. legend

The Jataka Stories
of Buddha

Thai Buddhists follow the teachings of Buddha. Four hundred years after Buddha died, someone wrote down some of his stories in stone. These stories are called the 'Jataka Stories.' The Jataka Stories had a very important function in the past. Buddhists used them to show people how to lead a good life. These traditional stories are now legends in Thailand. The heroes in a lot of these stories are monkeys. One well-known Jataka Story features a monkey, a crocodile, and a river.

The Jataka Stories

crocodile

river bank

river

A long time ago, a monkey lived alone on a river bank. He was a very strong monkey. In the center of the river there was a small area of land. On this land there was a lovely garden with trees that provided food for the monkey. There was also a large stone halfway between the river bank and the garden. Although it seemed impossible, every day the monkey stepped from the river bank onto the stone. Then he stepped from the stone to the garden. He did this to collect food from the trees in the garden.

One day, the monkey was in the garden and a crocodile laid down on the stone. The crocodile wanted to catch the monkey and eat him. At first the monkey wasn't aware of the crocodile. But then he looked closely at the stone and realized that it was different. "Hello, Mr. Stone. How are you?" said the monkey. The crocodile quickly answered without thinking, "I'm fine. I'm going to eat you." Then the monkey said, "Very well. Open your mouth." The crocodile had to close his eyes when he opened his mouth. So the monkey carefully stepped on his head and then safely onto the river bank. The crocodile lost his dinner that day. The lesson of the story is: always take time to think carefully before you answer a question.

CD 1, Track 06

Word Count: 316
Time: _____

Vocabulary List

banquet (2, 7, 8, 16, 18)
cake (2, 15, 16, 18)
demon (10, 11)
festival (2, 12, 15, 16, 18)
four meters (16)
hero (3, 8, 10)
karma (3, 12, 18)
legend (3, 8, 10, 11, 12)
mischievous (4)
monkey (2, 3, 4, 7, 8, 10, 12, 13, 15, 16, 18)
shrine (2, 12)
tradition (3, 8, 12, 16)